Let's Make a

Sandwich

by Mari Bolte

NORWOOD HOUSE PRESS

Norwood House Press

For information regarding Norwood House Press, please visit our website at:
www.norwoodhousepress.com or call 866-565-2900.

PHOTO CREDITS: page 4: ©Jose Luis Pelaez Inc / Getty Images; page 7: ©New Africa / Shutterstock; page 8: ©George Kuchler / Shutterstock; page 11: ©Anton27 / Shutterstock; page 12: ©Image Source / Getty Images; page 15: ©Olga Nayashkova / Shutterstock; page 16: ©MaraZe / Shutterstock; page 18: ©OlesyaSH / Shutterstock; page 19: ©Chatham172 / Shutterstock; page 21: ©Rosa Herrara; page 23: ©Rosa Herrara; page 25: ©Rosa Herrara; page 27: ©Rosa Herrara; page 28: ©Rosa Herrara

Hardcover ISBN: 978-1-68450-779-5
Paperback ISBN: 978-1-68404-752-9

LIBRARY OF CONGRESS CATALOGING-IN-PUBLICATION DATA
Library of Congress Cataloging-in-Publication Data has been filed and is available at catalog.loc.gov

353N—082022
Manufactured in the United States of America in North Mankato, Minnesota.

Contents

Americans eat 300 million sandwiches every day!

CHAPTER 1

All about Sandwiches

Sandwiches are the perfect quick meal. They include soft, chewy bread, hearty layers of meat, slices of cheese, veggies, and flavorful condiments. Everything you could want is squeezed between two slices of bread.

Bread's not necessary for the ultimate sandwich! Roll up the ingredients in a tortilla. Or try a lettuce leaf or cheese wrap. Sandwiches can fit into almost any kind of diet!

People have been baking bread for more than 10,000 years. They have been eating meat and vegetables for even longer. But it took a while for people to combine them into one meal.

People in the Middle East and Asia cooked **flatbreads** over fires. They used them to scoop up food to eat. In 500 BCE, or around 2,500 years ago, records show that Persian soldiers topped their flatbread with cheese and fruit.

A **rabbi** named Hillel lived in Jerusalem around 2,000 years ago. He began a tradition during the Passover holiday. He placed herbs and meat on a piece of flatbread called matzah. Then, he topped the creation with another piece of matzah. This was the first record of a sandwich. Today, making a Hillel sandwich is part of many Jewish people's traditions.

Sandwiches with just one slice of bread are called open-faced. They are easy to eat with one hand.

European people in the Middle Ages used old, stale bread called trenchers as plates. Food was piled on top. The juice from the food softened the hard bread. At the end of the meal, the trencher was eaten too!

More than 60 sandwiches got their names in America. Po'boys come from New Orleans.

The sandwich did not get its name until 1762. Earl John Montagu lived in an English town called Sandwich. He liked to play games. He did not like to stop to eat.

The Earl of Sandwich asked for something he could eat while playing. He loved the stack of bread and meat the cook made. Other people did too! The popular dish was named the "sandwich."

Americans got their first sandwich recipe in 1840. Elizabeth Leslie put it in her cookbook *Directions for Cookery.* Her sandwiches had two thin slices of lightly buttered bread and a little mustard. Slices of cold ham were put between the pieces of bread. Leslie said to serve them for "supper or at luncheon."

The first sliced bread was sold in 1928. People loved the convenience. They quickly realized that a sandwich could be made in a moment, and by anyone. Even young children could put together a sandwich!

The first peanut butter and jelly recipe was written in 1901. During World War II (1939–1945), they became popular. Soldiers ate them on the go. They were so good, soldiers wanted them back home.

There's never a wrong time for a sandwich. The first American breakfast sandwich recipe was written in 1897. It used meat, bread, milk, egg, and butter.

The Egg McMuffin changed breakfast sandwiches in 1971. Cheese, ham or sausage, and eggs on an English muffin was instantly popular. McDonald's even started selling them all day in 2015.

People give their city's sandwiches their own spins. Whether you're eating a submarine, a po'boy, or a hero, you're enjoying a sandwich. People around the world love them too. Served on a baguette, the bánh mì is a blend of Vietnamese and French culture. Cubans blend ham, roasted pork, Swiss cheese, pickles, and mustard. Then, the sandwich is grilled until the cheese starts to melt. Tortas are Mexican street food. Some have salsa or tamales in the middle.

Parts of a Sandwich

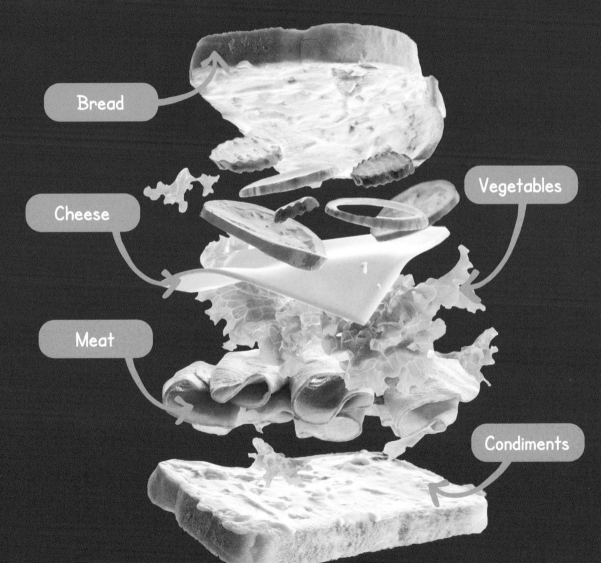

Bread

Cheese

Vegetables

Meat

Condiments

CHAPTER 2

Making sandwiches is a fun way to spend time with your family!

Making Your Own Sandwich

Choosing the right kind of bread is part of making the perfect sandwich. **Carbohydrates** in bread give the body fuel. Whole-grain breads have healthful carbs. They are full of **fiber**.

Most bread is made with wheat flour. Mixing and kneading wheat flour dough lets gluten develop. Gluten is a **protein**. It makes bread soft and chewy. Some people can't eat gluten, so there is also gluten-free bread.

Cold cuts are meats that have been **processed**. This makes them last longer or taste better. Cold cuts include deli ham and turkey. Bacon and pepperoni are other processed meats.

Salting and smoking are the two most common ways of processing meat. Salt and smoke both dry the meat out a little. This keeps bacteria from growing and helps the meat stay fresh longer. Smoke also adds a nice flavor.

Lunch meat is high in sodium. Sodium is a mineral found in salt. It helps the cold cuts stay fresh longer. People need small amounts of sodium to move their muscles. But too much sodium can cause health problems. Choosing lower-sodium deli meat can lessen that risk.

Meat is also high in protein. Protein is good for us! It helps our bodies heal and grow. It also carries oxygen around the body. And it's a great energy source.

Delis can slice meat and cheese to any thickness you want.

Meat is not the only protein option, though. Nuts and beans are full of plant-based proteins. They are also lower in fat and **calories**. When they are blended into nut butters and hummus, they become smooth and easy to spread on sandwiches.

There are around 2,000 kinds of cheese.

16

Cheese is another type of **preserved** food. It all starts with milk. Good bacteria is added to create lactic acid. Rennet is also mixed in. This encourages the milk proteins to stick together. Then, the milk **curdles**. The solid pieces are called curds. The leftover liquid is called whey.

The whey is drained off. Next, the curds are cut into smaller pieces and cooked. Salt is added, and more whey is drained off. Then, the curds are pressed into a cheese shape before being aged. In the end, the amount of cheese totals about one-tenth of the original amount of milk.

The type of milk, what the animal ate, and what kind of bacteria was used can change how cheese tastes. The longer a cheese ages, the more flavorful it becomes.

Of all the sandwich spreads, mayonnaise is the most popular in America.

Condiments are spices, sauces, spreads, or other ingredients that give sandwiches more flavor. They can be spread or sprinkled on. Mayonnaise is popular. It is made of oil, acid, and eggs. Normally, oil and vinegar do not mix. But egg yolks have fat. The fat binds oil and vinegar together. It also is what makes mayonnaise creamy.

Mustard is a spicy sauce made from mustard seeds. The seeds are mixed with water, vinegar, salt, and spices. Then, they are blended until smooth. You can also eat mustard greens! The whole plant is edible.

Pickling is a way to preserve fresh vegetables, including cucumbers, for a long time.

Pickles are a popular condiment too. They are usually made with cucumbers. The cucumbers are put in a brine. Brine is a mixture of water, vinegar, salt, and spices. The brine can be sweet, salty, sour, or spicy. Many vegetables can be pickled. Pickled radishes, peppers, onions, and carrots are good on sandwiches.

Some pickles are **fermented**. They are preserved through a chemical change. Yeast or bacteria turn the starch and sugar into acids. Sauerkraut, kimchi, and dill pickles are all fermented.

Fresh vegetables can give a sandwich crunch. They are also high in fiber. The more veggies you add, the more healthful and delicious your sandwich will be. Tomatoes, lettuce, and onions are classic additions. Cucumbers, peppers, and alfalfa sprouts are nice too! Avocado can add a creamy texture. Grilled eggplant or mushrooms can replace meat.

Lettuce can be used to make a wrap too. Lettuce has very few calories and is nutritious. It also adds a nice, fresh crunch. Many Asian countries use lettuce wraps instead of bread. Try using Asian condiments, like soy sauce or sriracha, on your next sandwich.

Some people use tortilla wraps instead of bread. They may think they are a more healthful choice. But that's not always the case. Wraps usually have less fiber and more calories, carbs, fat, and sodium. They are still a delicious choice, though. And they come in a variety of colors and flavors.

Materials Checklist

- ✓ French bread roll or soft hoagie roll

- ✓ condiments, such as mayonnaise, mustard, hummus, or oil and vinegar

- ✓ butter knife

- ✓ serrated knife

- ✓ sliced meat, such as turkey, ham, roast beef, or grilled tofu or mushrooms

- ✓ sliced cheese, such as cheddar, Muenster, or provolone, or a dairy-free alternative

- ✓ vegetables, such as lettuce, onions, tomatoes, and cucumbers

21

Because of their shape, hero sandwiches are also known as submarine or sub sandwiches!

CHAPTER 3

In the Kitchen!

Now that you know what goes into sandwiches, it's time to make your own! The hero is a delicious and easy sandwich with ingredients that can be mixed and matched.

1. If your bread is unsliced, ask an adult to use a bread knife to cut it. Using a serrated knife on bread easily cuts through a crusty outside and a soft inside.

2. Open the bread on your workspace, with the cut side up. Spread condiments on both sides.

23

3. Evenly distribute cheese over the bottom piece of the bread. It's okay if the cheese overlaps the edge a little.

4. Top the cheese with meat. If you're going meat-free, place mushrooms or grilled tofu.

5. Spread vegetables over the meat.

6. Place the top piece of the bread on the sandwich.

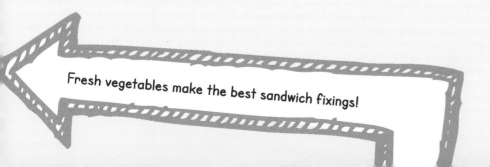
Fresh vegetables make the best sandwich fixings!

7. If necessary, gently press down on the top of the bread. This will help your sandwich stay together.

8. Ask an adult to cut the sandwich in half with the serrated knife. Enjoy it right away, take it to go, or share it with a friend. Then, start thinking about your next sandwich!

More Ways to Stack Up

Congratulations! You have made a sandwich. Now see if there are ways to make it even better. Use any of these changes and see how they improve your sandwich.

- Toast your sandwich for some buttery crispness. With an adult's help, melt 1 tablespoon of butter in a pan over medium heat. Set the sandwich in the pan. Use a pot lid, plate, or another pan to press the sandwich down. When the bottom of the sandwich is crispy, add more butter to the pan and flip the sandwich over. When it's toasted on both sides, remove from heat. Then, eat it!

- Bread, meat, cheese, and condiments come in many different flavors. Try herbed bread, spicy cheese, or garlicky meat. Add a condiment you have never tried. Maybe you'll find a new favorite!

Glossary

calories (KAL-uh-reez): units of energy

carbohydrates (kar-boh-HY-drayts): sugar molecules; along with protein and fat, carbohydrates are one of three main nutrients in foods and drinks

curdles (KURD-uhlz): when proteins bind together and separate from water

fermented (fer-MEN-ted): when yeast or bacteria have turned sugar into acid

fiber (FY-buhr): the parts of a plant your body can't digest or absorb

flatbreads (FLAT-bredz): thin, flat bread usually made without yeast

preserved (pri-ZURVD): altered during preparation, such as baking, freezing, or drying

processed (prah-SEST): having been changed from one form into another through special preparation

protein (PRO-teen): a complex molecule that provides structure and support to cells

rabbi (RAB-bye): a Jewish teacher or religious leader

For More Information

Books

Brundle, Harriet. *The Beginning of Bread*. Minneapolis, MN: Bearport Publishing, 2021.

Marsico, Katie. *Powerful Proteins: Strong Kids Healthy Plate*. Ann Arbor, MI: Cherry Lake Publishing Group, 2021.

Solheim, James. *Eat Your Woolly Mammoths!: Two Million Years of the World's Most Amazing Food Facts, from the Stone Age to the Future*. New York, NY: Greenwillow Books, an imprint of HarperCollins Publishers, 2022.

Websites

Discover the History of the Sandwich (https://www.pbs.org/food/the-history-kitchen/history-sandwich/) Explore the story behind sandwiches.

Three Pickling Recipes from Around the World to Make with Your Kids (https://www.pbssocal.org/education/three-pickling-recipes-around-world-make-kids) Get the low-down on pickles and how they're made—then, make them yourself!

Watch Kids Try 100 Years of Sandwiches (https://www.delish.com/food-news/news/a49142/watch-kids-try-100-years-of-sandwiches/) Watch kids try sandwiches and learn what their favorites fillings are.

Index

About the Author

Mari Bolte has worked in publishing as a writer and editor for more than 15 years. She has written dozens of books about things like science and craft projects, historical figures and events, and pop culture. She lives in Minnesota.